INSPIRATION QUOTES
ADULTS COLORING BOOK

Copyright © 2020 by Mason Kay

All rights reserved. No part of this publication may be reproduced,distributed or transmitted in any form or by any means including ,photocopying,recording or other electronic or mechanical methods.

This Coloring book Belongs to:

_____

_____

_____

_____

Color test Page